Contents

✔ KU-513-040

Introduction	4
Oceans and seas of the world	6
Ocean currents	8
How are waves made?	10
Make a storm in a soup bowl	11
Tides	13
How boats float	14
Floating around the world	16
Do things float higher in salt water?	17
Clothes for sailing	18
Which material is waterproof?	19
Finding a way	20
Use the stars to find North and South	21
Make a beam from a lighthouse	23
The key to life in the sea	24
Investigating spines	25
Moving quickly in water	26
Investigating fish shapes	27
Dolphins and whales	28
Going deeper	30
Make a model submarine	31
Animals of the deep	32
Abandon ship!	34
Dangerous animals	36
Life raft	38
Conserving energy	41
Rescue	42
Testing parachutes	43
Glossary	46
Index	48

Introduction

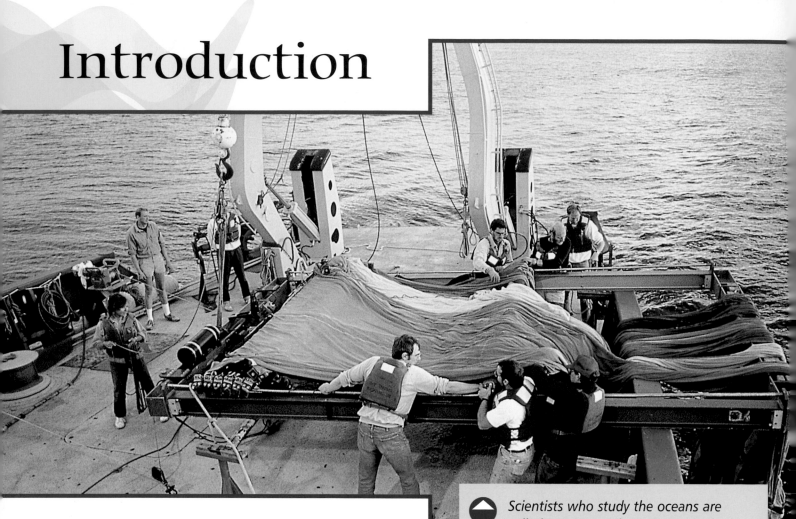

What's it like to set sail across the sea?

Have you been on a boating lake, perhaps in a canoe or rowing boat? The water was probably calm and the shore was never far away. Now imagine setting sail across the sea. You step on board your boat, which is ready to leave the harbour. The engine roars, the propeller turns, and off you go. Soon the land disappears from view and all you can see in the distance is water.

The keys to survival

People have sailed on the seas and oceans for thousands of years. The first reason for sailing was probably to catch fish. Later, people used boats to explore along the coasts. Eventually some people, such as the Polynesians and the Vikings, crossed the water to settle in distant lands. Today, many

Scientists who study the oceans are called oceanographers. Some study the ocean floor. Some investigate the chemistry of seawater. Others look at currents, waves and tides, and some study ocean plants and animals.

people work on boats, including fishing boats, oil tankers, cargo ships and liners. Some people make expeditions across the seas and oceans, to study their wildlife, search for oil and make discoveries about how the ocean currents flow.

More than two-thirds of the Earth is covered by sea. This watery part of the world is a vast place. We are going to see how people have learned to survive making journeys across the sea, and look at some of the many living things for which the sea is home.

Discovering with science

For thousands of years people have investigated their surroundings and made discoveries that have helped them survive. About 400 years ago, a way of investigating called the scientific method was devised, to help us understand our world more clearly. The main features of the scientific method are:

1 Making an **observation**

2 Thinking of an idea to explain the observation

3 Doing a test or experiment to test the idea

4 Looking at the result of the test and comparing it with the idea

Today the scientific method is used to provide explanations for almost everything. In this book you can try some science activities and find out about the science that helps people travelling across the seas and exploring sea life to understand the conditions and the creatures they may meet. In the activities you may use the whole of the scientific method or just parts of it, such as making observations or doing experiments. But you will always be using science to make discoveries.

Are you ready to find out how people survive at sea? Turn the page to find out about the oceans and seas of the world.

Explore how waves are made.
Page 11

Test floating in salt water.
Page 17

Find waterproof materials.
Page 19

Use the stars to find directions.
Page 21

Make a lighthouse beam.
Page 23

Investigate water resistance.
Page 25

Investigate fish shapes.
Page 27

Make a model submarine.
Page 31

Find out about the heartbeat.
Page 41

Test air resistance.
Page 43

Oceans and seas of the world

Just over two-thirds of the Earth's surface is covered by salt water. The largest areas of this water, between the continents, are called oceans. Areas of salt water closer to the land, or partly or completely surrounded by land, are called seas.

The Pacific, the Atlantic and the Indian Oceans are so large that each is divided into two parts – the part that is in the Northern Hemisphere and the part that is in the Southern Hemisphere.

You may have heard the saying 'to sail the seven seas'. It comes from past times, when sailors said there were seven oceans: the North and South Atlantic, the North and South Pacific, the North and South Indian Ocean, and the Arctic Ocean. (Parts of what they called the South Atlantic, the South Pacific and the South Indian Ocean make up what we call the Antarctic Ocean today.)

Arctic Ocean

North America

Atlantic Ocean

Tropic of Cancer

Caribbean Sea

Equator

Pacific Ocean

Tropic of Capricorn

South America

People on the oceans and seas

It would be possible to spend your whole life at sea, provided that you visited land occasionally to stock up on food and drinking water. However, people don't live at sea. They may visit it for some hours, days or months, to catch fish. They may travel across it for weeks, on holiday, or to transport oil and other goods between countries. Some people spend time at sea living on oil rigs, which are anchored to the seabed. Oceans and seas are also used for sport, and there are sometimes yacht races across oceans or around the world.

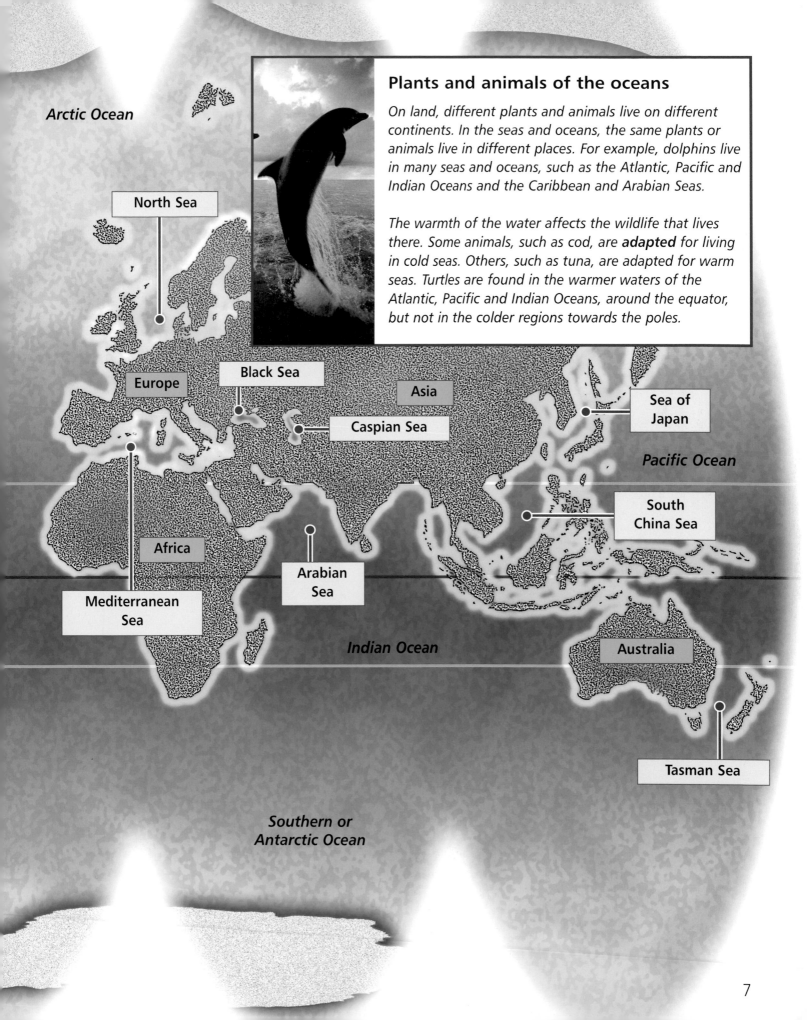

Arctic Ocean

North Sea

Plants and animals of the oceans

On land, different plants and animals live on different continents. In the seas and oceans, the same plants or animals live in different places. For example, dolphins live in many seas and oceans, such as the Atlantic, Pacific and Indian Oceans and the Caribbean and Arabian Seas.

The warmth of the water affects the wildlife that lives there. Some animals, such as cod, are **adapted** for living in cold seas. Others, such as tuna, are adapted for warm seas. Turtles are found in the warmer waters of the Atlantic, Pacific and Indian Oceans, around the equator, but not in the colder regions towards the poles.

Europe

Black Sea

Asia

Caspian Sea

Sea of Japan

Pacific Ocean

Africa

South China Sea

Arabian Sea

Mediterranean Sea

Indian Ocean

Australia

Tasman Sea

Southern or Antarctic Ocean

Ocean currents

The water in the oceans is never still. Winds blow on the surface, setting up currents in the upper layer of the water. In most oceans, these currents move in circular paths called **gyres**.

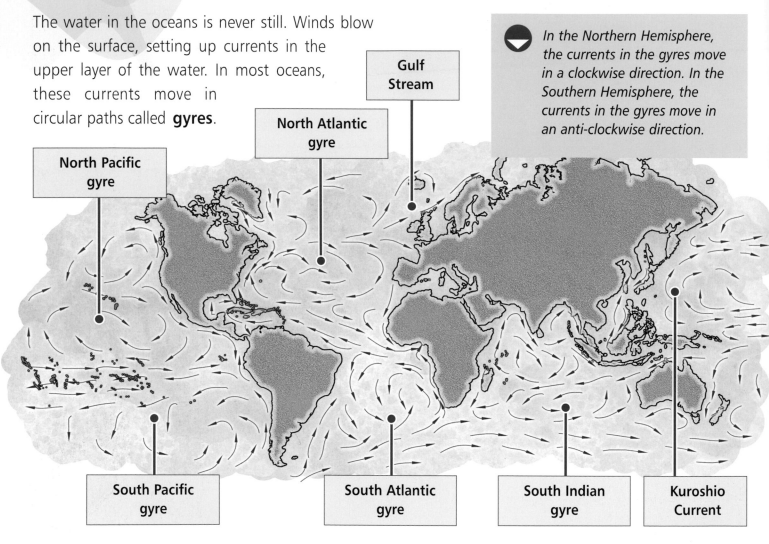

Gulf Stream

North Atlantic gyre

North Pacific gyre

In the Northern Hemisphere, the currents in the gyres move in a clockwise direction. In the Southern Hemisphere, the currents in the gyres move in an anti-clockwise direction.

South Pacific gyre

South Atlantic gyre

South Indian gyre

Kuroshio Current

In the Northern Hemisphere, the North East Trade winds blow the water to the west, and the Westerlies blow the water to the east. These winds set up the currents in the North Atlantic gyre and the North Pacific gyre.

In the Southern Hemisphere, the South East Trade Winds and westerly winds known as the Roaring Forties set up the currents in the gyres in the South Pacific, South Atlantic and South Indian Oceans. The speed of most ocean currents is about 10 kilometres a day.

Warm and cool currents

The Sun's rays heat the Earth most strongly at the equator. This means that water in the oceans at the equator is warmer than water to the north and south. Currents flowing from the equator are currents of warm water. Currents nearer the poles carry cooler water.

How the Earth's spin affects the currents

The turning of the Earth affects the water currents. If you look down on the North Pole of a globe and turn the globe in an anti-clockwise direction, you are making it turn like the Earth. On the surface, the Earth is always turning towards the east. As the Earth turns eastwards, the water in the North Atlantic and North Pacific gathers in large amounts on their western sides. These large amounts of water push strongly on the water to the north of them and make the currents that are travelling north move at speeds of 100-160 kilometres a day.

In the North Atlantic this fast-moving current is called the Gulf Stream. In the North Pacific the fast-moving current is called the Kuroshio Current. Both currents are also helped on their way by the wind.

Current complications and dangers

Other things that affect the way ocean currents move include the temperature of the water and the amount of salt it contains. The movement of the currents is very complicated. They don't just move across the surface but up and down in the oceans too.

While ocean currents can help people sail along, they can also cause great danger. Where two ocean currents meet, they may crash into each other and cause large waves.

 This large wave has been made where two ocean currents meet. These currents flow off the coast of Oregon, in the northwest USA.

How are waves made?

Most waves on a sea or an ocean are made by the wind. The size of the wave depends on three things: the distance over which the wind blows across the water (this is called the fetch), the length of time the wind blows, and the speed of the wind.

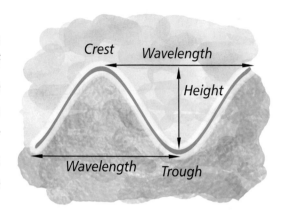

Crest · Wavelength · Height · Wavelength · Trough

*Every wave has a **crest** and a **trough**. The height of a wave is measured from its trough to its crest. Wavelength is the distance between two crests or two troughs.*

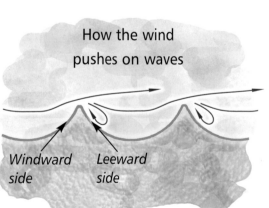

Ripples

How a wave builds up

A very gentle wind makes small waves called ripples, with rounded crests. The ripples stay rounded and smooth because the water surface is pulled in by forces in the water. These forces exist between the water molecules and produce **surface tension**, which makes the water surface seem to have a thin skin.

As the wind increases, it pushes the crests further apart and makes the wavelength longer. Now gravity becomes more important in shaping the wave, pulling down the water between the crests. There are two sides to a wave crest – the windward side, where the air pushes with a strong force, and the leeward side, where the air pushes with less force. This difference in the way the air pushes on the wave crest makes the crest even more pointed.

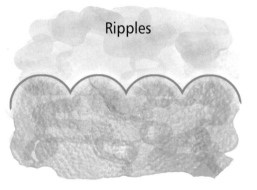

How the wind pushes on waves

Windward side · Leeward side

When the sides of the crest make an angle of 120 degrees with each other, surface tension can no longer hold the water surface on the crest like a skin and it breaks up. When this happens, the crest forms a white cap. A sea with white wave crests can be a danger to a small boat. The waves may turn the boat over.

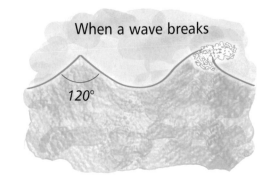

When a wave breaks

120°

Make a storm in a soup bowl

You can make observations on waves by creating some yourself in a soup bowl full of water.

You need a soup bowl with a broad rim, water, paper and pencil.

1 Fill the bowl with water and put it near the edge of the table.

2 Sit down so that you can bring your mouth close to the rim of the bowl.

3 Blow gently and look at the pattern of waves made in the water. Look for the way they cast shadows on the bottom of the bowl.

4 Draw the pattern you have seen.

5 Blow again more strongly, and draw the pattern.

6 Try blowing for different lengths of time, and draw the patterns.

7 When the water has settled, make a large number of very short, very strong blows. This should cause a chaotic wave pattern, which may splash your face!

Sketch the pattern you see in the water.

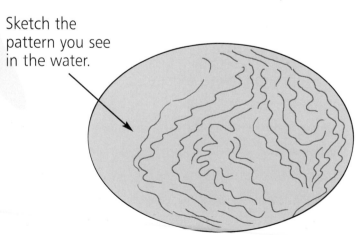

11

Waves on the beach

Often the wind makes waves with a low crest and very long wavelength. They move across the water, making the surface rise and fall as they go. This movement of the surface is called a **swell**.

When the waves in a swell reach the shallow water of a beach, their wavelength becomes shorter and their height increases. If the slope of the beach is gentle, the wave crests rise and break gradually to form **foam**. If the slope of the beach is steep, the wave crests rise quickly and the wave tips over and plunges down, making large amounts of **spray**.

How waves may break on a gently sloping beach

Gently sloping beach

How waves break on a steep beach

Steeply sloping beach

 It is safer to launch and land a boat on a gently sloping beach, because the waves tend to be smaller.

Safe harbours

As the wind plays a large part in making waves, places that are sheltered from the wind have smaller waves and make safer places to launch and land boats. Harbours are built in more sheltered places along a coast.

Freak waves and tsunamis

Freak waves occur very occasionally in storms. In a storm, the wind pushes on the water surface and makes waves with high crests and deep troughs. If the waves are made against the flow of a fast-moving current like the Gulf Stream, more water is pushed into them and they rise even higher. Freak waves may reach a height of 24-30 metres – large enough to sink a supertanker.

Another kind of huge wave occurs when a volcano erupts under the sea or there is an earthquake. It is called a tsunami. Out at sea, a tsunami may be less than 1 metre high, but as it moves towards land it becomes a wall of water over 30 metres high.

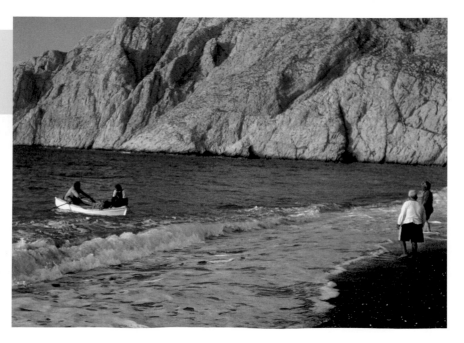

Tides

The **tides** are the movement of the sea up and down the shore. They are caused by the pull of gravity of the Moon and the Sun on the water in the Earth's oceans. The Moon's pull of gravity tugs the ocean water into a bulge where the Earth is closest to the Moon. On the other side of the Earth, a similar bulge of water develops.

Every day, as the Earth rotates, the bulge of water affects different parts of the coastline, causing the tide to rise up the shore. As that part of the coastline moves away from the position where the bulge occurs, the tide moves down the beach.

Twice a month, as the Moon goes round the Earth, the Sun's gravity pulls on the Earth's water in line with the Moon's gravity. This makes the tides rise higher and fall lower than at other times.

Currents near the shore

When the tide moves towards the shore, water can rush between islands and **sandbanks**, making strong currents. Similar currents occur in the opposite direction as the tide moves away from the shore. These currents can push a boat or ship onto a sandbank, or dash it against rocks and sink it.

How the Moon's gravity causes tides

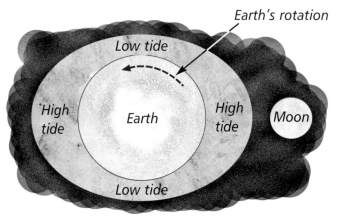

Earth's rotation

Low tide

High tide — *Earth* — *High tide* — *Moon*

Low tide

How the Sun's gravity affects tides

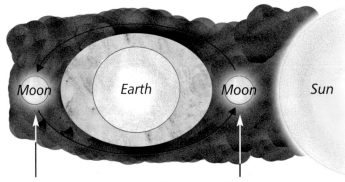

Moon — *Earth* — *Moon* — *Sun*

Twice a month the Sun, Moon and Earth are in line and the tides are at their greatest.

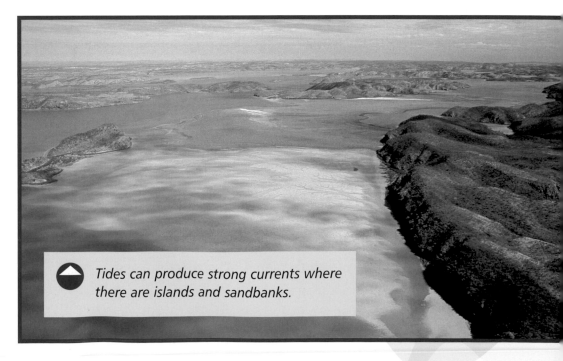

Tides can produce strong currents where there are islands and sandbanks.

How boats float

When a boat is on the beach, its weight pushes down on the ground. Once the boat has been pushed into the water, another force acts on it. This force is called the **upthrust**. It is due to the push of the water, but where does the push come from?

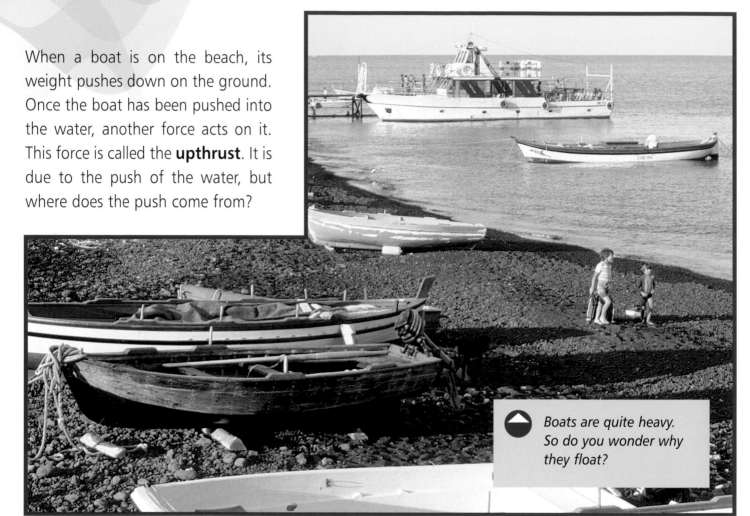

Boats are quite heavy. So do you wonder why they float?

When an object is placed in water, it pushes some of the water out of the way. You can easily see this happen if you fill a cup to the brim with water, place it in a saucer and put an apple in the water. The apple floats in the water but, in order to do so, it pushes out some water so that it can get in. This water spills over into the saucer.

If you weigh the apple and then weigh the water in the saucer, you will find that both weigh the same. As weight is a force and upthrust is a force, this means that the force of the upthrust pushing up is the same as the force of the weight pushing down. This balance of forces makes the apple float.

An apple floats in a cup of water. The water it pushes out of the cup weighs the same as the apple.

Any object that floats, such as a boat or a ship, has an upthrust pushing on it that is the same as its weight or greater than its weight.

If an object sinks, its weight is greater than the upthrust pushing on it. If you repeat the experiment with the apple, cup and saucer, but replace the apple with a ball of modelling clay, you get a different result. The ball sinks. The weight of the ball is much greater than the weight of water it displaces.

However, if the same piece of modelling clay is reshaped to make a hollow boat-shaped object, it floats. The new shape has a larger area in contact with the water, and so it pushes more water away. But its weight has not increased very much because the hollow is only filled with air. The weight of the air and the modelling clay in the boat is less than the upthrust, and so the boat floats.

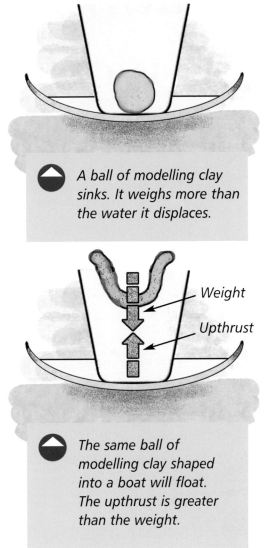

A ball of modelling clay sinks. It weighs more than the water it displaces.

Weight

Upthrust

The same ball of modelling clay shaped into a boat will float. The upthrust is greater than the weight.

If you could repeat this experiment with steel, you would get the same result. Steel boats float because the weight of the steel and the air inside the boat is less than the upthrust.

When fully loaded, a large ship displaces thousands of tonnes of water.

Floating around the world

 A ship sails out of port in Hamburg, Germany, along the River Elbe into the North Sea.

All materials, such as air, water and rock, are made of tiny particles that can only be seen by using powerful microscopes. In air and other gases the particles are free to move around. In water and other liquids the particles stay close together and slide over each other. In rocks and other solids the particles are stuck together. This idea of particles helps to explain what happens when a boat floats around the world.

Imagine that a boat starts its journey on a river in Northern Europe. In this cold water the particles come very close together. Each particle pushes on the boat and together they make a strong force, so that the boat floats high in the water.

When the boat enters the sea, it floats even higher. This is because particles of salt in the seawater add their pushing force to that of the water particles.

As the boat travels south and into the **Tropics**, the water becomes warmer and warmer. The particles in warmer water are more spread out and so they push with less force on the boat and it floats lower in the water.

Finally the boat sails into a river in a tropical country. The water is warm but does not contain salt to give an extra push. The boat floats even lower.

A boat that is overloaded is in danger of sinking if it is caught in a storm. In the nineteenth century Samuel Plimsoll introduced a way of knowing whether a boat was safely loaded. Plimsoll lines, on the side of a boat, show the safe levels for the boat to float in different kinds of water.

Plimsoll lines

TF — Tropical Freshwater
F — Freshwater (i.e. river water)
T — Tropical seas
S — Summer seas
W — Winter seas
WNA — Winter, North Atlantic

Do things float higher in salt water?

When scientists read information, they sometimes carry out experiments to check if it is correct. Use this experiment to check the information on page 16.

You need water, a measuring cylinder, two clear plastic beakers, spoon, salt, two plastic straws, marker pen, modelling clay.

1 Pour exactly the same amount of water into each beaker, so they are both about two-thirds full.

2 Add salt, a spoon at a time, to the water in one beaker until no more will dissolve. You can tell this has happened because salt crystals will be present at the bottom of the beaker.

3 Make scales on the straws by putting marks on them at half-centimetre intervals.

4 Make two identical pieces of modelling clay and fix one to each straw. Check that the straws float upright in the water without salt.

5 Move one straw to the salt water and look at the scale on each straw. Does the water level come to the same mark on each scale?

Clothes for sailing

The body needs to keep warm at all times. For people sailing in tropical seas, the weather may be so warm that only shorts and T-shirts are needed. Any exposed skin must be coated in **sun block**, to stop **ultraviolet** rays from the Sun damaging the skin. In cooler seas, thicker clothes should be worn to keep in the body heat.

Wet-weather clothes

If only light showers are expected, coats or jackets made from water-repellent material may be sufficient to keep you dry. These materials are made from fibres coated in chemicals called silicones. They make water drops roll up and slide off the material. Gaps between the fibres let out water vapour in sweat, to keep the body comfortable. These materials are widely used for cagoules and anoraks.

In a storm, heavy rain and waves would push water through the gaps between the fibres of water-repellent clothing and you would be soaked. Instead, you need clothes made from waterproof material. Its fibres are coated with substances such as oil or rubber, which block the air spaces between them.

Fluorescent patches on hood glow when light shines on them. They help rescuers find shipwrecked people at night.

A strobe light sends out flashes of light to show where the person is.

Whistle can be used in fog.

Flare gun is used to send a light high into the sky to attract attention.

Life-jacket inflates to keep the wearer afloat.

High collar and adjustable cuffs and ankle fasteners keep out water.

Waterproof clothing for stormy seas is called foul-weather gear. As there is also a danger of shipwreck in a storm, the foul-weather gear includes equipment and materials to help people who need to be rescued from the sea.

Which material is waterproof?

You need different types of material used for clothing, scissors, kitchen towel, measuring cylinder, water, clock.

1 Look at the materials and decide which will stop water passing through.

2 Cut a square from each type of material. All the squares should be the same size.

3 Cut squares of kitchen towel slightly smaller than the squares of material. Make sure the kitchen towel squares are all the same size.

4 Put a square of material over a square of kitchen towel. Pour a certain amount of water into the measuring cylinder, then pour it onto the material.

5 After 2 minutes, remove the material and examine the kitchen towel. Has it taken up the water?

6 Repeat steps 4 and 5 with the other materials.

7 Divide the pieces of material into a waterproof group and a non-waterproof group.

8 Which materials could be used for making waterproof clothes?

*You could continue your investigation by considering that waterproof clothes also need to be **flexible**. Test each material that you found to be waterproof, by bending and unbending it a number of times and then checking to see if this has made it less waterproof.*

Kitchen towel square should be slightly smaller than square of material.

Finding a way

The first people to sail the seas used many observations to guide them. They observed the direction of the wind, the direction of the currents, the patterns of the waves, the saltiness of the water, the types of clouds in the sky, and the directions in which the sea birds flew.

Wherever sailors went, they recorded the positions of features on coasts, the depth of the water, and the occurrence of sandbanks and low tide. All this information was used to make maps, which are carried on board all kinds of ships and boats today.

Stick charts

Sailors in the South Pacific made maps called stick charts, using shells and lengths of cane. The shells showed the positions of islands, and the cane pieces showed the currents. Sailors memorized the stick chart before they went to sea.

The compass and sextant

A map is only useful if the sailors know their position. A compass helps them to find the direction in which they are sailing, but their exact position in the sea is more difficult to work out.

In clear weather, a sextant can be used to measure the height of the Sun above the horizon. By looking in special tables for this measurement and the time it was taken, the position of the ship can be found. The sextant can be used when land cannot be seen, and so its invention enabled sailors to explore further out across the seas.

 *A sextant has a mirror and an eye glass, with a light **filter** to protect the eye. The sailor moves the mirror along the sextant arm until it reflects the Sun onto his view of the horizon. A scale on the sextant arm gives the height of the Sun.*

Use the stars to find North and South

At night, the positions of the stars can help sailors find the direction in which they are sailing.

You need a clear view of the night sky – preferably away from street lamps, an adult to accompany you.

In the Northern Hemisphere

1 Look into the sky and find the constellation called the Plough or Big Dipper. You can also think of it as a pan.

2 Look for the two stars farthest from the 'pan handle'. (Think of them as A and B.)

3 In your mind, measure the distance between A and B.

4 In your mind, make a line from A and B out into space. Make it about five times the distance between A and B. At this point you should find a star called the Pole star. It is the direction of North.

In the Southern Hemisphere

1 Look into the sky and find the constellation called the Southern Cross.

2 In your mind, measure the length of the longest part of the cross.

3 In your mind, extend a line from the bottom of the cross into space. Make this line about four and half times the length of the long part of the cross. Look down to the horizon at this point and you will be looking South.

N

Northern Hemisphere

Pole star

Plough or Big Dipper

A

B

Southern Hemisphere

Southern Cross

Pointer star

Long edge x 4.5

Pointer star

Horizon line

S

GPS

GPS stands for global positioning system. It is a system of **satellites** which allows you to find your position anywhere, on land or sea. There are many satellites in orbit around the Earth, including 24 that constantly send out signals about their position.

A person using GPS carries a receiver, about the size of a mobile phone. When it is switched on, it searches for signals from four of the 24 satellites. The signals are sent into a computer in the receiver and the position of the person is shown on a screen. This can then be used with a map, to help the person plot their journey.

GPS is widely used by ships and boats, but it can break down. It is then that older methods of finding a way, such as using a sextant or looking at the stars, have to be used.

A GPS receiver is a useful tool for people on an expedition.

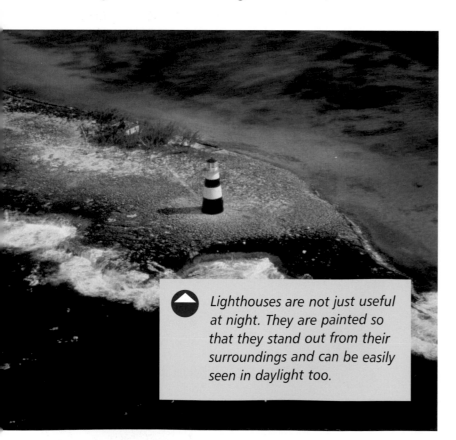

Lighthouses are not just useful at night. They are painted so that they stand out from their surroundings and can be easily seen in daylight too.

Coastal waters

Out at sea, sailors must battle with currents and winds to stay on course. Near the coast, they must be careful not to run their ships onto rocks just below the water surface. Many hazards near the coast are marked with **buoys**, which float in the water above them.

At night the outline of the coast is difficult to see. On many coasts there are lighthouses, which show sailors where the coast is and also help them find their position on a map. Each lighthouse sends out a beam of light for a certain length of time, as marked on the sailors' maps – so sailors can identify which lighthouse they are near.

Make a beam from a lighthouse

The lamp in a lighthouse stays on all through the night. A group of **lenses** turn around it to send out a beam. A lens is not used in the simple design here. However, you may like to improve the design and use a magnifying glass.

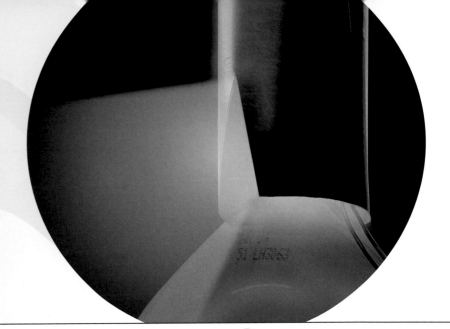

You need a 1.5V battery, a switch, a 3V bulb, three wires, a plastic drinks bottle, sticky tape, some black card.

Warning!
To avoid the bulb blowing, make sure it has the same or a higher voltage than the battery.

1 Make an electric circuit as shown in the photograph, with the bulb taped to the top of the bottle.

2 Make a black cover, with a slit in it, to fit over the top of the 'lighthouse'.

3 Make the room dark and switch on the light in the lighthouse. Turn the top of the lighthouse. Can you make a beam sweep round the room?

Run one wire from positive end of battery to 'on' side of switch.

Run second wire from negative end of battery to base of bulb.

Attach card cover with slit.

Run third wire from switch to base of bulb.

Tape bulb to top of bottle.

The key to life in the sea

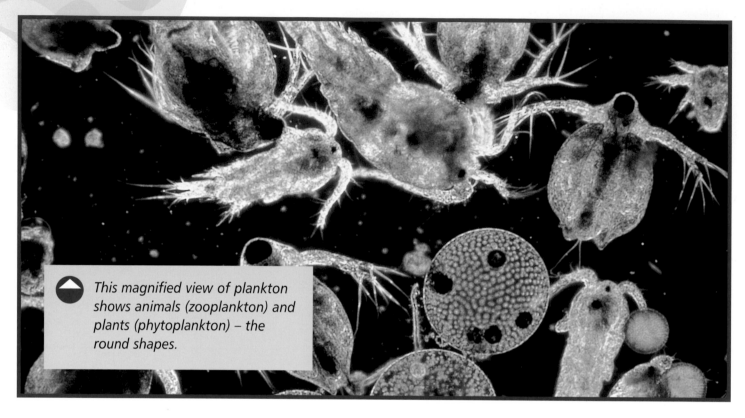

This magnified view of plankton shows animals (zooplankton) and plants (phytoplankton) – the round shapes.

The plankton is formed from huge numbers of very tiny plants and animals. They form a great cloud of microscopic life, which lies just below the surface of all oceans and seas.

The plants in the plankton

The microscopic plants are called **algae**. They have tiny bodies. Many are made from just one **cell**, and others are made from groups of cells. Inside each plant is a green **pigment** called chlorophyll. It traps energy from sunlight, and the plant uses this energy to make food.

As rays of sunlight shine down through the water, they lose their energy and become dimmer as they go deeper. The plants need bright light to make food, and so they must stay near the water surface.

Some algae have drops of oil in them, to help them float. Others have spines. These help slow down the plant as it sinks, and also catch upward-moving currents, to bring the plant back to the surface.

Animals in the plankton

Huge numbers of tiny animals feed on the algae. Many are tiny shrimp-like animals called copepods, but there are young crabs, lobsters and starfish too. The plankton is a nursery for many small animals and many fish lay their eggs there. The tiny animals are eaten by larger animals, such as comb jellies and small fish. These are eaten by larger fish, which may then be eaten by dolphins. The way the animals are linked together through feeding is called a food chain. So, all the animals in the food chains in the sea depend on the food the algae make.

24

Investigating spines

You can investigate the effect of spines on sinking by letting model algae fall through a thick liquid made with wallpaper paste. The models sink more slowly in this than they would in water, so it is easier to compare their sinking speeds. The force that slows down the sinking speed is called water resistance. It depends on the shape of the sinking body.

You need wallpaper paste (non-allergenic), a tall plastic bottle, scissors, modelling clay, stopclock.

 +

1 Ask an adult to mix the wallpaper paste. It should be quite clear yet quite thick. Also ask them to cut the neck off the plastic bottle.

2 Pour the thick liquid into the bottle.

3 Divide the modelling clay into several balls, all the same size. Leave one ball alone but make models of spiny algae with the others. Make one model with two spines, one with three spines, and so on.

4 Predict which model will sink the fastest and which the slowest.

5 Drop each model in, in turn, and time its fall if possible. If the models fall too quickly, make models from smaller pieces of modelling clay and try again.

6 Compare your results with your predictions.

Time the fall of each model.

Moving quickly in water

If you try to walk through water in a swimming pool, you will find it slow and tiring. When you swim, you move much more quickly and easily. Many fish swim much faster than us, to catch food and avoid **predators**. Their spindle shape allows the water to flow smoothly over their body, so that they can travel quickly.

Most of a fish's body is packed with **muscle**, to move its sides and its tail to and fro. This movement of the body and tail pushes the fish through the water. This is a much more efficient way of swimming than using arms and legs as we do.

As someone swims, they have to turn their head occasionally to bring their mouth and nose out of

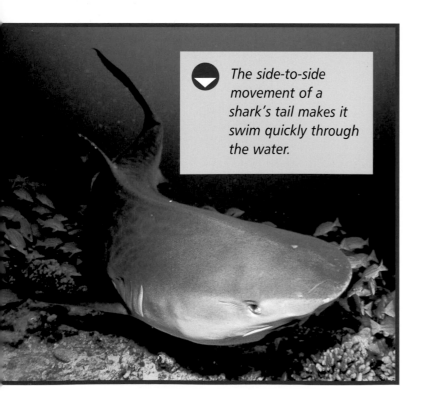

The side-to-side movement of a shark's tail makes it swim quickly through the water.

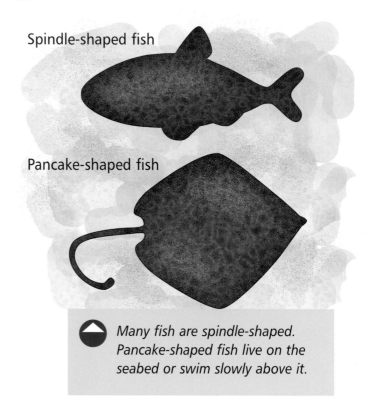

Spindle-shaped fish

Pancake-shaped fish

Many fish are spindle-shaped. Pancake-shaped fish live on the seabed or swim slowly above it.

the water so that they can breathe. A fish does not have this problem. It has **gills** inside its head. They allow it to breathe underwater by taking **oxygen** from the water and giving out **carbon dioxide**.

Moving up and down

A person has to swim hard to go deeper in the water, but many fish can rise and sink in the water without using the muscles in their tail and sides. They have an organ in their body called the swim bladder, which holds a gas that is released from the blood. When the fish wants to sink, it takes gas back into the blood and the swim bladder shrinks. This makes the fish less **buoyant** and it sinks.

When the fish wants to rise in the water, it releases more gas into its swim bladder. This makes the fish more buoyant and it rises in the water.

Investigating fish shapes

Sometimes scientists use the same equipment to make two or more investigations. In this activity you use the same materials as on page 25, but this time to investigate how shape affects the way an object moves. Some fish are spindle-shaped and some are pancake-shaped. Which shape do you think would help a fish move faster? Try this investigation to find out if you are right.

You need wallpaper paste (non-allergenic), a tall plastic bottle, scissors, modelling clay, stopclock.

1 Follow instructions 1 and 2 on page 25.

2 Divide the modelling clay into three equal-sized balls. Leave one alone but use the others to make models of fish, one with a spindle shape and one with a pancake shape.

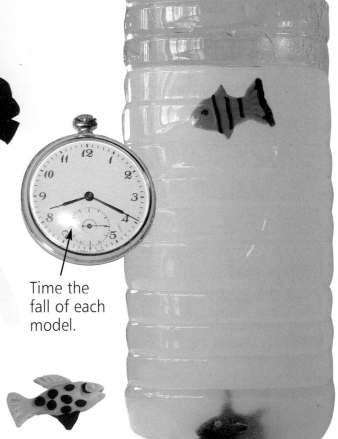

3 Predict which will sink the fastest and which the slowest, out of the ball and the two fish.

4 Drop each in turn into the liquid and time its fall if possible. If the models fall too quickly, make smaller ones and try again.

Time the fall of each model.

5 Make model fish shapes using your own ideas and compare their speeds.

Dolphins and whales

Dolphins often accompany a boat or ship as it sails along. They swim near the bow and at the sides of the vessel and sometimes leap out of the water, in a playful way. Occasionally the crew may be lucky enough to see a whale swimming by. Dolphins and whales are adapted for life in water, but must return to the surface to breathe air.

Fish-like mammals

Dolphins and whales are sometimes described as fish, because they have the spindle shape of a fish – but this is wrong. Dolphins and whales are **mammals**, like us, and this gives them two problems that fish do not have. All mammals obtain the oxygen they need from air, and have **lungs** to let them do this. They must also keep their bodies warm. By contrast, fish obtain their oxygen from water and have gills to let them do this. Their body temperature can change with the temperature of the water, without harm.

Regularly, throughout the day and night, whales and dolphins must return to the water surface to breathe. They have nostrils on the top of their heads. This allows them

Dolphins have a long, slender snout and a streamlined body, so they move smoothly through the water.

to float at the water surface as they breathe, and not to have to rise out of the water. When the whale or dolphin dives again, its nostrils close to keep water out of the **airways**.

The skin of whales and dolphins has a layer beneath the surface which is filled with fat and oil. This material is called blubber. It is a layer of **insulation**. This means that it acts like a blanket, stopping heat from inside the body passing to the water. Without its layer of blubber, a whale or dolphin would soon die in a cold sea.

How they feed

All dolphins and some whales, like the sperm whale and killer whale, have teeth. They use their teeth and jaws to grab hold of prey, but do not use them for chewing.

Some whales do not have teeth. They have large flaps which hang down from their upper jaw like curtains. The flaps are called **baleen** and the whales that have them are called baleen whales. The humpback whale and the blue whale are two examples.

There are bristles on the edges of the baleen plates and they make a **filter**. The whale takes a large amount of water into its mouth. The water may contain the whale's food of shrimps or fish. The whale then raises its tongue and forces the water out through the bristles. This leaves the food trapped on the inside of the mouth, ready to be swallowed.

 A humpback whale opens its mouth to feed. Humpback whales are found worldwide.

Going deeper

Before you dive, you breathe in deeply to take as much air into your lungs as possible. During the dive, you use up the oxygen in the air in your lungs to release energy, so that your arms and legs can move in swimming. As people are mammals, and cannot breathe underwater, you must return to the water surface to take your next breath. If you wanted to stay underwater a long time, you would need to carry a tank of **compressed** air on your back, to breathe as you were swimming along.

Submarines

In 1620, Cornelius Drebbel invented a craft that could take people underwater. It had leather bags, which were filled with water to make the craft sink. To make it rise, the bags were filled with air. This craft was the first submarine. By the end of the nineteenth century, ways had been found to make submarines move along through the water. They used **diesel** engines for moving at the surface, and battery-powered motors for travelling underwater. Submarines are very large craft, used mainly in navies but sometimes in exploration.

Submersibles

Smaller underwater craft called **submersibles** are used for many kinds of exploration, such as searching for new kinds of life in the deep oceans, investigating the rocks on the ocean floor, and examining the wrecks of ships.

Pressure

As an underwater craft makes a dive, the pressure of the water around it increases. This is due to the weight of water pushing down from above. On the inside of the craft is air for the crew to breathe. This air pushes outwards on the walls of the craft, but with much less pressure than the water pushing inwards. If the walls of the craft were weak, the whole craft would soon be squashed flat. All deep-sea craft must have strong walls to stand up to the pressure of the water.

Submersibles can take scientists right down to the ocean floor.

Make a model submarine

Submarines have spaces in them called **ballast** tanks. When the submarine is to dive, the tanks are filled with water. When it is to rise, compressed air is released into the tanks and this pushes out the water. Test this information by making a submarine that is really just one big ballast tank.

You need a plastic bottle with two holes cut in the side (ask an adult to do this), sticky tape, three coins, a piece of plastic tube about 50 cm long, modelling clay, a deep bowl of water.

1 Tape the coins next to the holes.

2 Put one end of the tube into the neck of the bottle and seal it in place with modelling clay.

3 Place the submarine in the water with the coins facing downward. Push it down in the water so that the air escapes and the submarine sinks.

4 Blow down the plastic pipe and observe what happens to the water in the submarine and to the submarine itself.

5 Try to make your submarine float just beneath the surface. You may have to nip the end of the plastic pipe together with your fingers and thumb at some time, to help you.

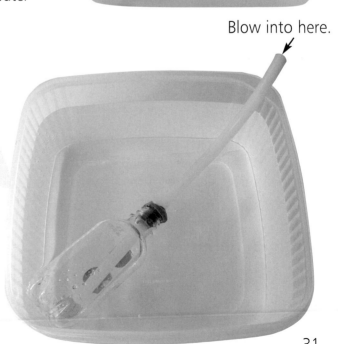

Submarine filled with water

Blow into here.

31

Animals of the deep

This deep-sea anglerfish is camouflaged, so that it is hard to see against the seabed. It lies in wait until its prey comes near. Then it wiggles a fleshy tip on its nose to attract the prey and opens its large mouth to catch it.

Around the coasts the water may be only a few tens of metres deep. A little further out it may be 200 or 300 metres deep. But right out in the oceans the water may be almost 11,000 metres deep. Even in the clearest waters, light can only reach down to 1,000 metres, so much of the deep ocean water is completely dark.

Without light there can be no plant life. Many animals living deep in the oceans rely on food sinking down from the upper waters. This food is the dead remains of other sea creatures. Some animals hunt for prey in the dark water.

Living in dark water

As there is no light from the Sun, many animals of the deep make their own. They have rows or patterns of spots, which give out light when special chemicals made in the animal's body use up energy from the animal's food. The light may shine weakly, so many deep-sea animals have large eyes in order to see it. They use the light to seek out prey and to find partners so that they can breed.

The deep ocean is a vast place and the chances of finding and catching food are small. Many deep-sea fish increase their chances of catching food by having large mouths. The jaws are lined with large numbers of sharp teeth to hold onto any food that is found.

On the ocean floor

Large areas of the ocean floor are covered in mud. The animals that live here have long legs (like the sea spider) or long spines (like sea urchins) to help them move along.

Sea spiders are not true spiders. They have many things in common with crabs and lobsters. There are a thousand different kinds.

There are seven hundred different kinds of sea urchin.

Hot black water streams upwards from a rocky pipe on the seabed known as a black smoker.

For many years scientists believed that every living thing on the Earth needed energy from the Sun in order to survive. Plants trapped the energy in sunlight and animals fed on the plants to get the energy they needed for life. In 1977 scientists using a submersible made an amazing discovery. They found rocky pipes rising 10 metres from a part of the seabed. Inside each pipe was an upward stream of hot water. The water was coming from a hot spring under the seabed. Chemicals in this water had formed the pipes. Other chemicals made the water black and it rose from the pipe tops like smoke rising from chimneys. Scientists found that bacteria were feeding on one of the chemicals in the black water. Worms and crabs were feeding on the bacteria, and these animals were being eaten by fish. All these living things were thriving because of the energy the bacteria took from the chemical – not because of energy from the Sun.

Abandon ship!

The most dangerous time for people at sea is when a ship sails into a storm. There are openings called hatches between the deck and the rooms below. Normally they are open, so that the crew can move more easily around the ship, but when a storm is due the hatches are closed. This is called 'battening down the hatches' and it stops seawater swilling down into the ship and making it more likely to sink.

Even when a ship has closed its hatches, it may be swept onto rocks by a strong current and its sides may be cut open. When this happens, water pours in through the holes and the crew and passengers prepare to abandon ship.

 These sailors are making their boat ready to sail safely through the storm.

Why a ship sinks

Ships float because their weight is balanced by the upthrust (see pages 14-15). The weight of a ship is made up from the weight of the materials it is built from, plus the weight of all the air it contains. When water rushes into a ship, air is pushed out. Water is much heavier than air so, as the ship fills with water, its weight becomes larger and larger. Eventually the upthrust can no longer balance such a large weight and the ship sinks.

Preparing to leave the ship

Ships are equipped with lifeboats and enough life-jackets for everyone on board. When a ship has just begun its journey, a lifeboat drill takes place. In this drill everyone is shown how to put on a life-jacket and which lifeboat they must go to if they need to abandon ship. This training helps to prevent a panic if the ship really has to be abandoned. A panic creates confusion and slows down the quick and orderly filling of the lifeboats.

Into the water

If someone jumps into the water, they must swim to keep themselves afloat. Swimming uses up energy and reduces the time the person can survive.

Some people may get their life-jacket on, but not be able to reach a lifeboat. They may survive by jumping into the water, as the life-jacket will help to keep them afloat. People who cannot even reach a life-jacket may survive if they throw an object that floats into the water and then jump in after it. When they come up, they can hold onto the floating object. The life-jacket and the floating object allow people to **conserve** their energy, as they do not have to swim, and so they can survive for a longer time in the water. This increases their chances of being rescued.

 At the start of their holiday, passengers on a cruise ship take part in a lifeboat drill.

Dangerous animals

 The Portuguese man-of-war cannot swim, but the wind may carry it long distances.

People swimming in the sea or floating in their life-jackets may encounter two main kinds of dangerous animal.

Jellyfish

Most jellyfish have a dome-shaped body from which hang tentacles. The jellyfish uses the tentacles to catch its prey. On the tentacles are stinging cells. They contain a poison that paralyses the prey, letting the jellyfish haul it up into its mouth. Some jellyfish, including a type called sea wasps, have such powerful poisons that they can kill people.

The Portuguese man-of-war is an unusual jellyfish. It has a large jelly bag full of gas, which helps it float at the water surface. The jellyfish was named after a type of ship, because its bag of jelly has a similar shape to the ship. The jelly bag is only about 15 centimetres long, but the tentacles, which hang down into the water, may reach a length of about 12 metres. If someone brushes against the tentacles, they will be stung, just as if they were prey. The stings are so painful that the person may be unable to continue swimming.

Usually the result of a jellyfish sting is an itchy or slightly painful rash. Treatment includes applying vinegar and using sticky tape to remove any fragments of tentacle that the jellyfish has left behind.

Sharks

There are many kinds of shark, but the six that have attacked people the most are the Bull, Nurse, Hammerhead, Great White, Mako and Tiger sharks. The Great White is up to 6 metres long.

How to avoid attack

Swim strongly

Sharks are lazy killers. They search for prey that is weak. Many fish swim in groups called shoals. If a fish is struggling to keep up with a shoal or is wounded and shaking its body weakly, then a shark will detect these movements and attack. Someone swimming in shark-infested waters should make strong movements and keep a regular rhythm. They should not splash about weakly, as this may make sharks think there is a weak or injured animal ready to be eaten.

Keep quiet

Sharks can be attracted by noise, so at times when they are feeding – dawn, dusk and through the night – keeping quiet may keep them away.

Keep together

If survivors floating in the sea are spread out, they make small targets for a hungry shark. In a group, they make a larger target, which sharks are more likely to leave alone.

Give it a shock

When a shark threatens to attack, people have survived by hitting it on the nose with a stick, slapping the water with their hands, or putting their head underwater and shouting.

Shark repellent

Some lifebelts used in tropical waters have a shark repellent on them. Travellers in shark-infested waters may carry shark repellent with them. However, they must use it as a last chance to stop an attack because, once it is used, it spreads out in the water and cannot be used again.

The Great White shark is considered the most dangerous of all.

Life raft

On this ship, the inflatable life rafts are stored in metal cylinders above the deck, ready for immediate use if the ship has to be abandoned.

Many ships and boats carry life rafts. A life raft can be packed into a small space so it does not take up much room on board. When it is needed, it can be thrown over the side and inflated. Many life rafts have a carbon dioxide cylinder, which blows up the **hull** automatically as soon as the raft hits the water.

The hull of the raft is made from one or more buoyancy tubes. Each tube is separate so that, if one tube gets a puncture, the others do not go down and the raft can stay afloat. A tube that arches over the hull also fills with gas. This makes a support for the canopy.

The canopy is made from a waterproof material and helps the people on the raft to stay dry. It is also made in a bright colour, which stands out against the colour of the seawater. This makes it easier for rescue helicopter pilots to see. If a few life rafts are being used, they should be linked together, so that they make a larger colourful object for pilots to spot.

The life raft

The life raft has a broad, low hull. This shape helps it stay the right way up, even when being tossed around by large waves.

*On top of the canopy is a light operated by a battery, so the life raft can be seen at night. But if the light goes out, there is still a chance that the raft may be seen by a rescue craft using a searchlight. There are **reflective** strips on the canopy, which reflect the light back to the rescue ship.*

Inside the life raft is an emergency pack, containing a range of useful equipment. There are paddles, which can be used to move the life raft over the water when it is calm. There is a bag, which can be used to bail water out of the raft. A repair kit contains patches of material, glue and stoppers, which can be used to mend leaks. There are flares, which can be used to signal for help. When a flare is shot high into the air, it produces a bright light.

Around the hull of the life raft is a lifeline. This can be used as a handle by anyone who is in the sea. They can hold on to the lifeline and move round to the ladders to climb on board.

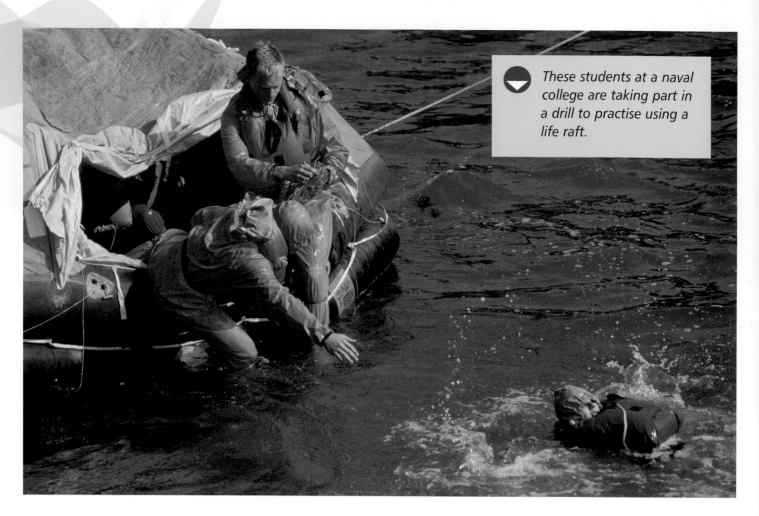

These students at a naval college are taking part in a drill to practise using a life raft.

Keeping healthy in a life raft

Two essentials for life are water and food. You may think that, being surrounded by water, people in a life raft would have plenty to drink – but you would be wrong. Seawater contains large amounts of salt. Although the body needs a certain amount of salt to stay healthy, too much will cause the **kidneys** and other organs to become damaged, and death may follow. Therefore, seawater must never be drunk.

The emergency kit of many life rafts includes a container of water, but this may not last long. People adrift in a life raft must conserve water, just as people do in a desert. They must ration the water so that everyone gets a little each day. They can also collect water when it rains, and when dew forms on the canopy of the raft. The dew can be soaked up with a cloth. This water does not contain salt.

There may be some dry food in an emergency kit, but this must only be eaten when absolutely necessary. The body uses up water when it digests food so, if there is little water on the raft, it is better not to eat.

People on a raft should rest as much as possible. Then they do not use up so much of the energy that their body has stored and they do not need to eat. In hot climates, resting stops people becoming even hotter and starting to sweat heavily. So resting also helps to keep water in the body.

Conserving energy

Your heart pumps blood around your body, carrying food and oxygen to all parts of the body. Much of the food and all of the oxygen is used to release energy. When we move, we use lots of energy and our heart beats fast to supply the muscles with their energy needs. In a life raft, you need to conserve energy by moving very little. Use your heartbeat as an indicator of energy use and see how it slows when you rest.

You need a clock, a comfortable place to lie down. +

1 Walk about for two minutes and then stand still.

2 Hold out your left hand and turn the palm upwards. Put the thumb of your right hand underneath the left hand, so it presses upwards on the wrist. Bring the first and second finger of your right hand down onto the wrist and feel for a place where the flesh throbs. This is the pulse.

Place fingers here to find the pulse.

3 Count the number of beats of the pulse in 30 seconds. Double the number of pulse beats you counted to find the number of beats in a minute.

4 Sit down for five minutes. Then repeat steps 2 and 3 while sitting. What do you find?

5 Lie down for five minutes. Then repeat steps 2 and 3 while lying down.

6 Compare the pulse beats after walking, sitting down and lying down. What do you find?

41

Rescue

All ships have a two-way radio, which is used to receive and send messages. The messages received come from coastguards, who work to keep people safe when they visit the shore or pass by in ships. The coastguards radio the ships information about changes in the weather and other ships in the area. The ships radio the coastguards to tell them their position and where they are going.

The radio operator on board a ship that is about to sink calls out 'May Day' and repeats it for as long as possible. 'May Day' is a signal of distress, which is known in all countries. It is really the French phrase 'M'aidez!', which means 'Help me!'

Rescue services

When coastguards hear the May Day signal, they try to find where it is coming from and send out rescue services. This may be a helicopter or a lifeboat or sometimes both. A helicopter crew can get a clear view of the sea as they fly over it. But a lifeboat crew may not be able to see a life raft, if the life raft and the lifeboat are both in troughs between very high waves. If this happens, the helicopter can help guide the lifeboat.

Flares

When people in a life raft can hear or see their rescuers approaching, they can attract attention by releasing flares, found in the emergency pack. Some flares shoot out smoke. They are used in daylight, as the smoke stands out against the sky.

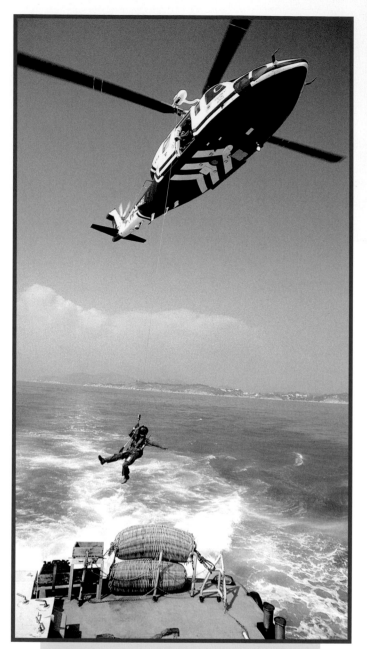

A rescue worker descends a rope from the helicopter onto the boat where someone is in difficulty.

Other flares for use at night shoot out coloured light, like a firework. One type of flare, which can be used at any time, has a parachute. When the flare is released it may rise as high as 90 metres. Then the parachute opens and the burning flare sinks slowly to the sea. This means that there is more chance that the flare will be seen.

Testing parachutes

When a flare with a parachute falls through the air, air pushes upwards on the parachute with a force called air resistance. If the air resistance is large, the parachute falls slowly. If the air resistance is small, the parachute falls quickly. Compare the air resistance of parachutes by making this fair test.

You need a plastic bag cut into different-sized squares, string, sticky tape, two weights such as metal washers.

1 Cut four pieces of string, all the same length.

2 Tape one end of each piece of string to a corner of the smallest piece of plastic.

3 Tape the other ends of the string to a weight.

4 Repeat steps 1-3 to make a parachute from a larger piece of plastic.

5 Drop the two parachutes from the same height and find out which one sinks faster.

6 Repeat steps 1-5 with another pair of parachutes.

7 Switch the parachutes round so that each one has been paired with all the others and work out which has the greatest air resistance and which has the least.

Tape string to washer.

Tape string to plastic.

All lifeboats are designed for travel in rough weather and carry special safety equipment.

Lifeboat

The kind of lifeboat that is sent out from the coast to rescue people is different from the lifeboats that are lowered from a sinking ship. It is designed to stay afloat in very rough seas.

A ship or boat may sink in a storm because the materials from which it was made split apart where they were joined and water gets in through the split. Sinking may also be caused by water swilling down open hatches into the hull. The materials used to make a lifeboat are very firmly joined so that they will not split apart in a storm. Also, when a lifeboat takes to the sea, all the hatches are shut. The firmly sealed joints and closed hatches trap air inside the lifeboat and this makes it unsinkable.

The heaviest part of the life boat is its engine. This is placed deep in the hull, where it pushes down strongly on the water. If a wave knocks the lifeboat over, the weight of the engine pushes down on the water again and makes the lifeboat return to its correct position, as the diagrams show.

How a lifeboat stays upright

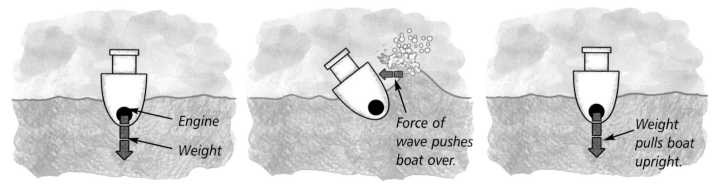

Engine
Weight

Force of wave pushes boat over.

Weight pulls boat upright.

Land ahoy!

Sometimes people adrift after a shipwreck are not spotted by rescue services. They must then look out for signs of land and paddle towards it.

- Fluffy clouds called cumulus clouds often form over land, so when these are spotted in a clear sky, land may be in that direction.

- Sea birds usually fly away from land in the morning and back to it in the afternoon. Paddling along the path of the birds may bring a life raft to land. If the sound of birds increases as you paddle, there is a good chance that land is not far away.

- Floating objects such as branches, leaves or even coconuts could indicate that land is not far away. It may be worth paddling in the direction that these objects seem to be coming from.

- If the colour of the sea changes from blue and green to yellow and brown, there may be the mouth of a river not far away. The change in colour is due to particles of mud and rock that have been washed out to sea from the river's mouth.

Cumulus clouds may be a sign of land.

The end of the journey

When people reach the end of a journey, they usually feel they have learnt a lot along the way. How did you get on, travelling over the oceans? Can you explain how a wave forms and how a black smoker is made, or name six dangerous sharks? Also along the journey you have had many chances to try out your science skills of observing, predicting and experimenting.

Algae in the oceans produce huge amounts of oxygen when they make food in the sunlight. The oxygen passes into the air and travels all over the Earth. Wherever you are reading this, you will be breathing in some oxygen that was made in the oceans – so, in a way, you can say that the oceans are helping you to survive at this moment.

Glossary

adapted with body features that make it easy to survive in certain places.

airways tubes inside an animal which allow air to pass to and from the lungs.

algae tiny plant-like living things that can only be seen clearly with a microscope.

baleen a substance in some kinds of whale, made from hair that is stuck together and formed into long flaps in the mouth. Sometimes called whalebone.

ballast a material used to control the way a submarine moves.

buoy a brightly coloured floating object, possibly with a light or bell, anchored above underwater rocks to warn boats and ships that they are there.

buoyant having the tendency to float.

carbon dioxide a gas produced by living things when they use oxygen to release energy from food to keep them alive.

cell a tiny structure that is capable of life. Most animals and plants are made from millions of cells.

compressed squashed into a small space.

conserve use something sparingly, so some is saved for use later if needed.

crest the highest point of a wave.

diesel a fuel which is changed into vapour and then squashed strongly in an engine, to make it explode and power the engine.

filter a structure which lets water pass through a fine mesh to separate any small solid particles from it. Some materials filter light, letting through only a small amount of light.

flexible able to bend a great deal.

fluorescent describes materials which take in light that shines on them and release some of it back into the air.

foam a mixture of gas and liquid. The gas forms a huge number of bubbles in the liquid.

gills a part of the body of fish and some other water animals, used for breathing in water.

gyre the circular path taken by the currents in most oceans.

hull the part of a water craft, such as a ship, that rests in the water.

insulation a material that prevents heat passing through it. Some insulation prevents electricity from passing through.

kidneys	parts of the body that remove wastes from the blood and let them leave the body in urine.		**satellite**	an object carrying electrical devices such as computers, radio transmitters and receivers, which moves in a path called an orbit around the Earth.
lenses	discs of clear glass or plastic which can be used to make light into a beam.		**spray**	small drops of liquid moving through the air.
life-jacket	a jacket made of material that will help a body float.		**submersible**	a craft which can travel underwater for short periods, e.g. a few hours.
lungs	parts of the body that take in oxygen and release carbon dioxide.		**sun block**	a cream which prevents the harmful rays of the Sun damaging the skin.
mammals	animals that have a fur, and whose females give their young milk.		**surface tension**	an effect made by the way water molecules hold together: the water surface seems as if it has a skin.
muscle	a part of the body that contracts (gets shorter) to make the body move.		**swell**	the rising and falling of large areas of the sea surface.
observation	looking at the way something is, or the way in which something happens.		**tide**	the movement of the sea up and down the shore, due to the Moon's pull of gravity.
oxygen	a gas found in air and also dissolved in water. It is used by nearly all living things to help keep them alive.		**Tropics**	the region between the Tropics of Cancer and Capricorn (see pages 6-7).
pigment	a substance that gives colour to the body of a living thing.		**trough**	the low point between two wave crests.
predators	animals that feed on other animals.		**ultraviolet**	a form of energy. It travels as waves, with a shorter wavelength than light, and cannot be detected by our eyes.
reflective	able to reflect light, and therefore easy to see if light shines on it in the dark.			
sandbank	pile of sand formed in the sea by the movement of water currents.		**upthrust**	a force that pushes upwards on any object placed in a liquid.

Index

air resistance 43
algae 24, 25, 45
animals 4, 7, 24, 32, 33, 36-7
Antarctic Ocean 6, 7
Arctic Ocean 6, 7
Atlantic Ocean 6, 7, 8, 9

beach 12, 14
birds 20, 45
black smokers 33
boats 4, 10, 12, 13, 14-15, 16, 20,
    22, 28, 34, 38, 42, 44
buoys 22

chlorophyll 24
clothes 18-19
clouds 20, 45
coasts 20, 22, 32, 44
compass 20
currents 4, 8, 9, 12, 13, 20, 22,
    24, 34

diving 30
dolphins 24, 28-9

Earth 8, 9, 13, 22, 33
energy 24, 30, 32, 33, 35, 40, 41

fetch 10
fish 4, 6, 24, 26, 27, 28, 29, 32,
    33, 37
flares 18, 39, 42
floating 14-15, 16-17, 24, 35, 36,
    45
foam 12
food 6, 32, 40, 41
food chain 24
forces 14, 25

GPS 22
gravity 10, 13
Gulf Stream 8, 9, 12
gyres 8

harbour 4, 12
hatches 34, 44

Indian Ocean 6, 7, 8
islands 13

jellyfish 36

Kuroshio Current 8, 9

lifebelt 37
lifeboats 35, 42, 44
life-jacket 18, 35
life raft 38, 39, 40, 45
light 18, 20, 22, 24, 32, 33, 39, 42
lighthouses 22, 23

mammals 28, 30
maps 20, 22
materials 18, 19, 38, 44
Moon 13

ocean floor 4, 30, 31 (see also
    seabed)
oceanographers 4
oil rigs 6

Pacific Ocean 6, 7, 8, 9, 20
parachutes 42, 43
plankton 24
plants 4, 7, 24
Plimsoll lines 16
Portuguese man-of-war 36

rescue 18, 35, 38, 39, 42, 44, 45
ripples 10
rivers 16, 45
rocks 13, 22, 30, 34, 35

sailors 6, 20, 21, 22, 34
salt water 6, 9, 16, 20, 40
sandbanks 13, 20
satellites 22
scientific method 4
seabed 6, 26, 32, 33
sextant 20, 22
sharks 26, 36-7
ships 4, 13, 15, 16, 20, 22, 28, 30,
    34, 35, 36, 38, 42, 44
sinking 15, 16, 24, 25, 34, 44
stars 21, 22
storms 12, 16, 18, 34, 44
submarines 30-1
submersible 30, 33
Sun 8, 13, 18, 20, 32, 33
surface tension 10
swell 12
swim bladder 26
swimming 26, 30, 35, 36, 37

tides 4, 13, 20
tsunamis 12

upthrust 14, 15, 34

water, drinking 6, 40
water, sea and ocean 4, 7, 8, 9, 32, 45
water resistance 25
waves 4, 9, 10, 11, 12, 18, 20, 39, 44
weather 18, 20, 42, 44
whales 7, 28-9
winds 8, 9, 10, 12, 20, 22, 36